New rules for massive success in 21st Century

New rules for massive success in 21st Century

HARISH MIGLANI

Published Internationally by

Pendown Press

Powered by Gullybaba.com

PENDOWN PRESS

Powered by **Gullybaba Publishing House Pvt. Ltd.,**
An ISO 9001 & ISO 14001 certified Co.,
Regd. Office: 2525/193, 1st Floor, Onkar Nagar-A, Tri Nagar,
Delhi-110035, (From Kanhaiya Nagar Metro Station Towards
Old Bus Stand)
Branch Office: 1A/2A, 20, Hari Sadan, Ansari Road,
Daryaganj, New Delhi-110002
Ph.: 09350849407, 011-27387998
E-mail: info@pendownpress.com
Website: PendownPress.com

First Edition: 2020

Price: ₹199/

ISBN: 978-93-89601-51-0

Layout Design: Pendown Press Publishing

CONTENT

Dedicated to all Success Lovers!

PREFACE

Can you ride a bicycle with only one tyre? Answer is a BIG No. That is the main reason I came up with the idea of 2 Big Steps.

Many people work very hard to achieve what they wished, but internally they feel it is really very hard to live in the world, at the same time they also think Hey God why only me!

With this mindset, they keep on going everywhere but reach nowhere Finally the last hope arises when they take the help of astrologer, but still nowhere. The reason is not in the stars.

ACKNOWLEDGEMENTS

Before I imprinted my thoughts on paper, I was just passionate to learn new things in life which could take me to the top of the world.

I wanted people to know what treasure of learning I had, but I had no idea where to start from.

Over time, with the support from my better half Mrs. Nidhi Miglani, with inspiration from my mentor Mr. Akshar Yadav, I was able to craft my ideas into paper.

But how to make it as a masterpiece was still a challenge, and destiny filled this big gap too when I met Mr. Dinesh Verma in an event in Delhi. I am delighted that I have been able to complete this journey.

I am extremely grateful to my father Mr. Somnath Miglani, who himself never took rest, and ensured many positive habits in me, without which I wouldn't be able to complete this book.

I am extremely grateful to my mother Mrs. Mahesh Miglani, who herself was always ready every day and night for mental support.

I am thankful to all other family members for being there as my motivation and especially my children, who had always cooperated with me during this entire journey. I had stolen a lot of time from them.

It has been a long journey, and I am really thankful to Mr. Dinesh Verma, CEO, Gullybaba Publishing House, and his entire team, specially Ritu, for their support and guidance throughout this entire journey.

ABOUT THE AUTHOR

Mr. Harish Miglani had a very humble background. He had to face lots of financial challenges till the age of 20. Apart from money, another big challenge before him was the direction of life. There was no clarity over what direction he should decide, what profession he should choose and how he should begin his career.

However, with inspiration from his seniors, he picked CA as a career choice and completed exams in the very first attempt in the year 2006. After becoming Chartered Accountant in the year 2006, Mr. Harish started a CA coaching institute in 2009 to give coaching to CA aspirants.

At the time of his practice and coaching to students, Mr. Miglani observed that there are people in the society who are intellectual, disciplined, but there is something that holds them all. And after he delved deep to explore that "something", he came to know that some people had big dreams, vision in life, but they don't know where to start. No action is taken by them. On the other hand, there are some people, who do not have big dreams, they are just involved in the game of survival. He is now engaged in transforming the lives of the people around him.

1
CHAPTER

WHY THIS BOOK?

There was a Sunday morning... I received a call. There was a beautiful voice of a girl, "Harish sir speaking?" I said, yes.. And then she started crying and after that nothing was beautiful because... she told me her brother has attempted suicide. The name of her brother is Sammy (Name changed for confidentiality) who is a successful chartered accountant and was my student 10 years ago. I still remember him as he was very brilliant student of his class.

After I stopped conversing with her, I started empathising with her. I started feeling her tears. The thoughts of that boy started coming to my mind like a movie...a sincere, intelligent, hard-working, and handsome as well.

He used to tell me, "Sir, you are my inspiration". My eyes misted over at his high academic standard and unhappy fate.

She had requested me to visit the hospital. I started for hospital.

When I visited him, he was lying on bed and his Left-hand was full of white colour dressings. When enquired, I came to know that he had put his hands on the main electricity passing through their terrace.

After some time, when doctors allowed me to have a word with him, then the conversation started like this: Sammy.... "Why did you do this? And his answers were very surprising and shocking to me...

He said, "I don't want to live anymore , sir". He could not continue his sordid saga because tears started rolling down on his cheers. Sensing all these, her sister intervened and continued. Turning her face towards me, she started telling the reason, " Sir, as you too will agree, he is very ambitious. He started his own business with three of his friends. Everything was hunky-dory till the time he was in India, with them. But, the day he flew to US to get some oversees assignment and stayed there for 6 months, the ulterior motive of his partners came to the fore. They would provide the wrong figure of the financial health of the company, put forged bills on expenditure and my brother had to pay heavily since he was so trustful towards his friends, and his busy time schedule in the US had left him with little time to check the veracity of the financial claims that they were making.

When he came back to India, he was dumbstruck to see the financial condition of his company. There was huge loan pending on my brother. They had duped my unsuspecting brother.

Seeing all these, Sammy lost his mental equilibrium. He started losing his sleep, and this state of melancholy remained for almost 6 months. Day before yesterday, he took this extreme step.

I was hearing all these with rapt attention. I could not have believed all these things, had he and his sister themselves not told me what went wrong with my dear student. I decided to improve him as a person, train how to take a situation(bad) head on and emerge triumphantly.

I talked to the parents of Sammy and expressed my willingness to do something for the greater good of my student. Both of his parents became ecstatic to know about my decision. Their eyes were clearly communicating the sense of gratitude for me.

After a few days of getting discharged from hospital, he, along with his sister, came to my office. He was clueless, what to do further in life.

Then the interesting story begins.... How I helped Sammy to transform his life. I suggested him to visit my office every Tuesday for the next 7 Tuesdays.

I shared with him the secret of living life not only with

success, but also with happiness and bliss, which I had observed and learned, in my life. The very purpose of writing my book is to save any Sammy take such extreme steps. The secrets of happy and blissful living are grouped in just 2 BIG STEPS explained in this book.

I have incorporated in this book all the insights and questions from Sammy with which you will relate to. All these are the excerpts from our weekly conversation with Sammy.

Before moving further, I want to ask you a question: Are you happy in your life? Because there is something you want to change in your life, otherwise you would not have picked my book. That "change" could be related to your financial, health business or anything like these.

2

CHAPTER

HOW TO GET BEST OUTOFTHISBOOK

Have you read so many books, but no one of them worked for you?

Then I would like to congratulate you because you have chosen a right and solution-oriented book.

It's my advice that if you really want to transform your life, then don't try to read the entire book at one go. First understand then implement, and then move to the next chapter of this book.

Forget about other books, this book is to the point and task-oriented.

Overall secret to success is just 2 BIG STEPS. Wonder? You read it right. While most of the books only address problems, and doesn't provide any solution, but in this book, there will ACTION LIST after every chapter.

In some places, I have given you some tasks e.g. filling the worksheet or some other tasks. It's my warning not to proceed further before completing the given task, otherwise reading this book will not get you where you actually want to go.

You will see, how Sammy's travel to different places along with me helped him get rid of his wrong beliefs that he had about life and success and how his life turned around after applying the 2 BIG STEPS propounded by me and incorporated in this book.

This little book is not just a book, it's a success manual, which will guide you step by step to achieve more and more in life.

At the end, I assure you, after reading this book and applying those 2 BIG STEPS, described in this book, you will definitely reach at next level in your life. HOWEVER, if you are struggling to find where to start with, you will also be able to lead your life to the right track.

> **Happy reading and I wish all the success comes to your way.**
>
> **–Harish Miglani**

Always remember

> **" Execution is more important than perfection"**
>
> **–Harish Miglani**

3
CHAPTER

MEANING OF SUCCESS

On 1st Tuesday Morning, I was expecting Sammy at the given time. I too had prepared myself accordingly, because he was too sincere to miss an appointment even by a minute or two. He came on time, touched my feet in such a way as if he was communicating with his body language that he has surrendered himself to me.

I drove him to a village area near my city. I asked him just to walk in the village for 10 minutes and come back. He was very curious about what will happen. I asked him to contain his excitement and just to observe the village for 10 minutes in a stretch.

By the time he was exploring and observing, I sat below the tree to avoid heat. I was wondering as some kids were playing cricket in the street and the ball was hitting the people who were passing through the street. They were also happily enjoying this. Some old-age persons were sitting under the tree, they were playing cards and discussing the recent political drama happening in the country.

After my prescribed time, Sammy returned with surprising expressions, and started speaking:

"Oh my God! There were some ladies pulling the water with the help of a rope from well, and they are facing so many difficulties just to get one pot of drinking water,

And he observed many difficult situations like that.

Now, I was about to give a task to him,.I said, "Sammy go again, but this time not just observe, you have to speak with them, what is their biggest wish of life right now."

This time he returned after around 1 hour, and here is what he observed there:

Ladies, who were pulling water, wished for water connections in their homes, so they don't need to come daily to take water like this.

Kids who were playing cricket, wished for victory in the cricket match they were playing.

Old-age persons wished pleasant weather so that their activities don't get disturbed.

In this way, every person was having a different opinion regarding their biggest wishes, but one common factor was that wish was driven by their present problems.

After telling me all these, Sammy abruptly asked me, "Why you brought me here?"

(Now my answer to Sammy is also a lesson for all the readers of this book.)

"To make you understand the true meaning of success", I replied. Because we always link our happiness or success to some kind of achievement, and this achievement may come in life after 6 months, may be in 2 years, or may be in 8 years time, or even more than that

But the true meaning of success is just to conquer the present challenge, and move to the next challenge. These series of challenges is called life.

I told him, Sachin Tendulkar is known as the greatest player of the century today, he has scored approx 35,000 runs in international cricket.

His approx. 35,000 runs are nothing but sum total of various innings which he played, in which there are some double hundreds, some hundreds and some fifties. Apart from these, it is also a sum total of some 30s, 20s or even 10s.

Yes, Sammy, he didn't score 100 in every match, no body can

When he used to play a match, he just focused to play well

in that particular innings only, he never played keeping his eyes on achieving maximum score in International Cricket.

Life is very much like this. In some challenges, you may not score 100s, you may have to settle for 10s or 20s. But, remember! Life will definitely give you chance to play another match. Forget what happens yesterday, move to the next challenge. Do not get carried away with(past) failures.

A big success is nothing, but just a total of small successes and some small failures as well.

Meaning of success can be very different for each person . For example, for an unhealthy and obese person getting into shape is success, whereas for a student getting good score is the only success.

Let me define success for you...No matter whatever meaning you have given to it, but success is not a destination to be reached. For me being successful means to be on the right journey, because...

> **If you are moving in the right direction, someday you will reach your destination.**
>
> **–Harish Miglani**

You can't claim to be successful now, if you have achieved something 10 years back, and now you have nothing. Simply put, you can not sit on your laurels.

In this world, real achievers are those, who didn't sit after one big accomplishment. They always get aspired for the next level to reach.

> **"Success means doing the best we can with what we have. Success is the doing, not the getting; in the trying, not the triumph. Success is a personal standard, reaching for the highest that is in us, becoming all that we can be."**
>
> **– Zig Ziglar**

> **"Success is an attitude or a mental state in which you have to be in every single day and moment "**
>
> **–Harish Miglani**

Action Points

Identify present challenges (those who are preventing you from achieving your dreams) of life, and come out of this. It may be related to your Health, Finances, Career, Business or relationships etc.

1. ____

2. ____

3. ____

4. ____

4
CHAPTER

WHY SUCCESS IS NOT HAPPENING

> **If you are living for survival game, one day even survival will become difficult.**
>
> **–Harish Miglani**

There are so many reasons for not getting success, but first of all we have to come out from 'Game of Survival' and think beyond this.

Game of Survival

When I asked Sammy, "Sammy, Why you were doing that business?" He was shocked, but immediately smiled and said, "Sir, you are joking, I had to do it", Sammy replied with full energy, moving hands on his long hairs.

Why you had to do it ?

You could do something different, you could work like a consultant, trainer or entrepreneur.

Sammy replied, "Sir, I had to do it because of constant income stream, that made easy for me to pay my bills, my rent, my cost of living."

Hey Sammy, sit on this luxury sofa, have coffee and listen to me calmly now.

I said to him, "Most of the young people do the same mistake, you are also one of them. People are intentionally or unintentionally force themselves into game of survival, yes Sammy, survival is the only driving force for most of people in whatever they do."

> **"It's not enough to have lived.**
> **We should be determined to live**
> **for something."**
>
> **–Winston S. Churchill**

Living Life without Purposes

Do you know what are the real mistakes they are doing?

For Sammy and hundreds of thousands of other young people, earning money is the only purpose of their life, They choose occupation accordingly, they work in that direction only. But, the legends in the society don't think about money, (I am not saying don't earn money, in fact earn money in abundance).

The legends are known for contributing the society, and then money flows like a rain on them. Mr. Bill Gates gave MS-Windows to the mankind, Mr. Mukesh Ambani gave JIO, Steve Jobs gave iphone and ipad and the list is never-ending. Legends always make life easy for mankind with their contribution.

On the contrary, the only target of common man is to pay the bills, EMIs, rent, etc. When they are able to pay it, they feel like achiever, as if they have done a life-enriching work.

For reaching at heights, you have to come out of this game of survival. Because this game will end up reaching nowhere and eventually one day even survival will become difficult.

Stephen Hawking said that you can not hold yourself at a position— either you are moving forward or backward. So, your dream should be of achieving next level always, and after reaching, again aspire for the next level.

Ask Yourself a Question

Am I just looking to pay my recurring expenses, or I am in the universe for something big?

Reasons of This Game

We all are born with big visions, a child wants to have a lot of money. He always looks for big celebrities and repeatedly admires them and also wants to become like them. However, sometimes society and surroundings limit our thinking to such levels.

Possible reasons of this conditioning of mind is:

- We see our parents or/and other relatives so much involved into this game.

- We see our neighbours are in this game.

- Due to media, because it is loaded with such news, where people are dying because of hunger, and not able to take medical treatment.

Apart from the reasons mentioned above, there are many more reasons also there, which make the mindset of people like this.

And this journey continues till a child becomes an adult. Now, an adult who wants to break that pattern is not able to come out because deeply he assumes that it is very difficult. We have to struggle too much to achieve the heights.

But in the upcoming chapters. I will be giving you the secret named as 2 BIG STEPS to come out from this game of survival.

5
CHAPTER

UNDERSTANDING 2 BIG STEPS

Everyone knows everything, still most of the people are not getting success. Why ?

Because most of the people only work on one aspect, not on other aspect. To get success, you have to continuously work on both the steps.

It was around 3 pm, and Sammy wanted to leave. But, I asked him, "You have to stay for another 30 minutes to understand the concept of 2 BIG STEPS".

You can't skip any of the steps. These 2 steps are like a 2 tyres of bicycle. They will go side by side. You can't stop one and move another.

And I started to introduce those 2 BIG STEPS to Sammy. Here is excerpt of my teaching:

You want to earn 5 crores in a month. But deep inside, you believe that it is not possible, or you believe that money is the root cause of all problems. Then, it's dead sure you will not be able to make it, or even if you made 5 crores by chance, you will lose it in short span of time.

On the other hand, some people only work on affirmation, vision board, and positive thinking. They set reminders to remind them to stay positive. They put stickers on their tables and walls etc. But they don't take actions to achieve them.

> **"Your mind is a magnet. If you think blessings, you attract blessings. And if you think of problems, you attract problems. Always cultivate good thoughts and always remain positive."**

The whole idea is that you have to work on both aspects side by side, and these 2 BIG STEPS are:

1.   Tune your psychology

2.   The massive actions

But how to tune your psychology right, and how to take

actions, there are some tricks to do it, over the period of 10 years, I have observed all these tricks, and they will definitely work for you as well.

In the upcoming part of the book, I will be providing all those tricks to apply in your life.

STEP-1 : TUNE IN YOUR PSYCHOLOGY/ MINDSET

Part-I Fine-tune your belief Set

That was 2nd Tuesday when Sammy was about to come at 9 am. As usual, he reached on time and I gave him a folded paper and asked him to take out his pen. I instructed him, when you will open this paper there is a question written on it. You have to write the answer of this question in 3 seconds only.

He immediately unfolded it, and wrote the answer within 3 seconds. I took the paper from him and narrated the below story to him.

As a man was passing the circus, , he suddenly stopped, as he saw elephants. He was amazed to see that these huge creatures were being held by only a small rope tied to their front leg. No chains, no cages, nothing

It was obvious that the elephants could, at any time, break away from their bonds but for some reason, they did not.

He saw a trainer nearby and asked why this giant animal just stood there and made no attempt to get away.

"Well," trainer said, "When they were very young and much smaller, we used the same size rope to tie them, and at that age, it's enough to hold them. As they grew up, they are conditioned to believe they cannot break away. They believe the rope can still hold them, so they never try to break these ropes."

The man was amazed. These animals could at any time break free from their bonds but because they believed they couldn't, they were stuck right where they were.

Now the question arises: how many of us go through life hanging onto a belief that we cannot do something, simply because we failed at it once before?

I started explaining to him.

What we are today, is largely because of our belief

system. We may be rich or poor, sick or healthy, slim or fatty, intelligent or average and optimistic or pessimistic. Whatever we are, we hold a very strong belief related to it.

> **Man often becomes what he believes himself to be.**
>
> **–Mahatma Gandhi**

Let's open the paper Sammy, I asked him.

When we opened the paper he wrote 5 million. The question was, "What is the annual income you really want to touch in future in your life?"

But answer will not be the same for everyone, someone will write it as 1 million or even someone may write it 1 billion.

Let's again focus on the question.

What is the annual income you really want to touch in future in your life?

See the important word in the above question— it is future, but everyone thinks it differently.

Point to consider is that, here question is not of right or wrong. The real question is why everyone thinks differently with such a high degree of variation. See it's 1 million to 1 billion.

Our beliefs set an upper limit on our thinking. If we will not think beyond a point, how we can manifest it?

How Beliefs are Made?

Actually, they are made by the people we trust most. Means our surroundings, in most the cases our parents, relatives or teachers.

When a child is born, he is blank.

Then I asked from Sammy, please tick the statement (which are given below) which you had listened in your childhood.

And the statements are:

	How a child interprets it?
Why are you becoming so careless? Why you can't greet your elders? Why you can't speak with confidence? Why you get angry with little issues?	"I am careless, not sincere, angry"
Why you wasted such hard-earned money?	Money is hard to earn.
Why you are so fearful?	I am fearful.

I am not saying don't question them. But, generally what parents do, they generalise a single incident. But children are not so enlightened and that's why they get affected by it. Eventually, they hold beliefs about such statements said for them.

What to do now?

You have to work on 2 aspects,

Firstly you should make empowering belief in future.

Secondly, you have to get rid of old disempowering belief.

I am giving you a trick so that in future you will be capable to safeguard yourself from disempowering beliefs.

Question yourself not others

Whenever something negative or disempowering is told to you, question yourself immediately and think, am I generally.........?

Let us understand it with the help of an example. Suppose you are a businessman, one day your client complains you that you always delay delivery of goods, ask from yourself, "Does this happen regularly or frequently? Answer yourself No. Even if it is yes, tell yourself— generally it is No. But, if it is increasing, I am capable to deal with it.

Give some reasons to support it. You will say, only few customers complain like it. In the last month, I received an appreciation letter from my very reputed clients. I had employed the skilled manpower and all my plants are modern and maintained professionally.

If you will not give such reasons, then your subconscious mind will take it as I am very unprofessional, who generally delays the delivery.

How to get rid of past Disempowering Belief

Our beliefs are like unquestioned commands, hidden commands you can say to best describe these. You do not know about these commands till the time you are not able to change your limiting beliefs. Unless you change your pre-conceived beliefs, you will lack that sense of certainty that allows you to tap the power that is within you. These are the beliefs that shape our action, feeling and thought.

Therefore, changing our (old) belief system is central to making any real and lasting change in our lives. Simply put, if we become able to overcome the boundary of our set belief pattern, we will definitely be able to upgrade our life and lead a life that we desire.

So, the million dollar question here is: How can we get away from our disempowering belief?

First of all make list of all such beliefs

Do it now, before moving further in the book.

Your language should be like this.

I have been told that ....

For example,

1. I have been told that I am not a good-looking person.

2. I have been told that money can't be earned easily.

3. I have been told that there is so much competition in the world, life is not easy.

Now, what to do?

Convert those negative statements into positive ones by questioning, adding a bit followed by a contradictory statement to your past disempowering belief.

For example,

1. I have been told that I am not a good-looking, person but my smile can kill millions.

2. I have been told that money can't be earn easily, but it is very easy to earn money and I know several persons who made millions of wealth very easily and in a fair way.

3. I have been told that there is so much competition in the world, life is not easy. But I have the courage to be unique and stand out in the competition.

Warning!

Don't mix the facts with beliefs. If a person has gained extra pounds, and he is overweight, this is a fact. Now, this can be reversed or not, is based on the beliefs of such person. If he thinks it is easy to be in shape, he will be. On the other hand, if he believes that once you gain weight, it is pervasive, then any remedy will not work to get slim.

> ## Action Points
>
> Speak the positive statement (which you have made as suggested above) loudly in front of mirror at least 3 times a day facing your own eyes.

Part-II Activating DMS (Decision Making System)

Unlocking mobile without password

A weird moment happened when, we both (me and Sammy) went to a coffee shop, after fine-tuning the belief set of Sammy. The bill amount was around Rs. 300, and I forgot to take cash, and I handed over my mobile to Sammy and asked him to pay through Paytm. He asked how to unlock it because it was password protected. I asked him to try again. He irritated, but remained silent about it, and again with a disagreed expression he replied, "Sirrr, how can I open it without knowing the password?"

But that was my weird way to teach him one of the most powerful lessons of life.

I again started preaching him...

A locked mobile can be logged in only through password, similarly, there is a tool to activate DMS (Decision Making System) in your mind.

He was looking at me, with a curious expression. I started telling an example.

Suppose you have a sum of Rs.2,00,000 in Fixed deposit as savings for your future. Suppose your friend comes to you and asks for money because he wants to travel abroad.

What will be your answer?

Off course NO!

On another scenario-

Suppose any of your family members needs medical treatment and they don't have another source of money.

> **"You can't make decisions based on fear and the possibility of what might happen."**
>
> **–Michelle Obama**

Now, will you spend those 2 lakhs?

In most of the cases, the answer will be in affirmative.

In the example discussed above, haven't you seen how fast you have made the decision?

But how?

Because it activates your DMS (Decision Making System) faster.

Let's understand it in detail.

Because you love your family, you care for them.

Isn't it?

There is a deep insight in this example

In the latter case your reason, or 'why' is stronger and this applies to every situation of life.

Let us say-You want to achieve something–a perfect body, billions in your bank account, topper in exams, BUT WHY.

Unless and until you are not clear about your why, you will take actions half-heartedly.

That is the power of WHY.

If you are delaying decisions, that doesn't mean you are dumb, or lazy.

It simply means that you haven't found your TRUE WHY till now.

What WHY can do for you

- WHY activates DMS

- WHY inspire you

- WHY keeps you on track

Now the question is-How to find your WHY

Finding why is very easy but you have to allow some time for yourself.

"After giving these insights, I allowed Sammy to leave and give homework to perform the action steps."

Action Points

Take a piece of paper and write- WHY you want to do what you are doing. For example

Q1. WHY you want to grow your business?

Ans. For money

Q2. Why money?

Ans. To make my family happy

Q3. How your family will be happy with money?

Ans. I will shift them in big house.

Q4. Why big house?

Ans. Problem of small house

And series of questions will continue like this

The whole idea is – WHY is not enough.

Your ACTUAL WHY is hidden behind several Why.

SO, FIRST FIND OUT YOUR ACTUAL WHY.

Part-III Upgrade your Proximity

It was the 3rd Tuesday. This time I asked him to stay at home, I drove to his home, and asked him to come with me.

He was very much energetic that day, because he was able to find "WHY" of his life. He requested for guidance from where he should start now. But no, I was in fear that after a few weeks, he can distract again. Therefore I started speaking, "Sammy! Get ready for some criticism in your life." He immediately replied, "Why Sir?", Atthat time, we were in front of zoo. We both went inside, bought tickets and entered in the zoo.

Why you brought me here? Sammy said. "Let's go and find lion", I replied almost instantly We found it and I asked Sammy to throw a piece of stone inside the boundary where lion was sleeping. He refused because it was illegal, and he also said he will roar.

> **"Proximity is Power."**
>
> **–Tony Robbins**

It's ok, I said to him.

Later on we both sat on a bench in zoo, where we both can see that lion. Today again it was a story to tell. And the story was....

Find the lion within

An ancient parable in the East is that a lioness was jumping from one hillock to another and just in the middle, she gave birth to a kid.

The kid fell down into the road where a big crowd of sheep was passing. Naturally he mixed with the sheep, lived with the sheep, behaved like a sheep. He had no idea, not even in his dreams, that he was a lion. How could he have?

All around him were sheep and only sheep. He had never roared like a lion; a sheep does not roar. He had never been alone like a lion; a sheep is never alone. She is always in the crowd – the crowd is cozy, secure, safe. If you see sheep walking, they walk so close together that they are almost stumbling on each other. They are so afraid to be alone.

But the lion started growing up. It was a strange phenomenon. He was identified mentally with being a sheep, but biology does not go according to your identification; nature is not going to follow your mind. He became a beautiful young lion, but because things happened so slowly, the sheep became accustomed to him, just as he became accustomed to the sheep.

The sheep thought he was a little crazy naturally. He was not behaving just right – a little cuckoo- and he went on growing. It was not supposed to be so. Pretending to be a lion! But they knew he was not a lion; they had seen him from his very birth. They had brought him up, they had given their milk to him. He was a non-vegetarian by nature— no lion is vegetarian, but this lion was, because sheep are vegetarian. He used to eat grass with great joy. They accepted these small differences, that he was a little big and looked like a lion. A very wise sheep said, 'It is just a freak of nature. Once in a while it happens.'

And the lion himself also accepted that it was true. His color was different, his body was different — he must be a freak, abnormal. But the idea that he was a lion was impossible! All those sheep surrounded him, and sheep psychoanalysts gave him explanations: 'You are just a freak of nature. Don't be worried. We are here to take care of you.'

But one day an old lion passed by and saw this young lion standing far above the crowd of sheep. He could not believe his eyes! He had never seen such a thing nor had he ever heard that in the history of the whole past a lion had been in the middle of a crowd of sheep but no sheep was afraid. And this lion was walking exactly like the sheep, grazing on grass!

The old lion could not believe his eyes. He forgot he was going to catch a sheep for his breakfast. He completely forgot breakfast. It was something so strange that he determined to catch hold of the young lion and find out what was happening. But he was old, and the young lion was young – he ran away. Although he believed that he was a sheep, when there was danger this much of the identification was forgotten. He ran like a lion, and the old lion had great difficulty in catching him.

Finally the old lion got hold of him. He was crying and weeping and saying, 'Just forgive me, I am a poor sheep. Please let me go.'

The old lion said, 'You idiot! You simply stop this nonsense and come with me to the pond.' Just nearby there was a pond. He took the young lion there. The young lion was not going willingly, he went reluctantly, but what can you do against a lion if you are only a sheep? He may kill you if you don't follow him, so he went. The pond was silent, with no ripples, almost like a mirror.

The old lion said to the young, 'Just look. Look at my face and look at your face. Look at my body and look at your body in the water.'

In a second there came a great roar! All the hills echoed it. The sheep disappeared; he was a totally different being – he recognized himself. The identification with sheep was not a reality, it was just a mental concept. Now he had seen the reality. The old lion said, 'Now I don't have to say anything more. You have understood.'

The young lion could feel a strange energy he had never felt before – as if it had been dormant. He could feel a tremendous power, and he had always been a weak, humble sheep. All that humbleness, all that weakness, simply evaporated.

(source: https://www.movemequotes.com/lion-sheep/)

A lion can forget his roaring capacity if it is in the group of sheep. We all are born to live with our fullest capacity. But our disempowering beliefs had prevented us from living to the full capacity.

> **"You are the average of the five people you spend the most time with."**
>
> **–Jim Rohn**

Upgrade Proximity

Proximity plays a very important role in success of a person. People you surround yourself will play a big part in the type of person you are.

Whether it be friends, family or colleagues, it is important to surround yourself with people who bring out the best in you.

You need to think about the person you want to be and surround yourself with the people on a similar mission to you, and who have a similar mindset to you.

You also need to cut out the negative people who drain you and keep you back.

It is like a powerhouse that lights you up when you are in dark but it also sometimes pushes you in those dark corners if not chosen wisely.

Proximity is the companion or your friends you choose to be with.

Some people become addicts not because their parents have offered/served them this with food, but it's because of their circle of friends they are with.

This is how proximity works.

If you want to turn your dreams and goals into a reality faster, you must get yourself in proximity with people who are playing the game at a higher level than you are.

Whether it's your business, health, finance or relationships- surrounding yourself with people who are already successful in that area allows you to model what is proven to work, helping you compress decays into days.

If you want to be successful, surround yourself with successful people and you will see the impact that will have on you.

> **"People can either inspire you, or drain you. Pick wisely."**
>
> **–Source : Internet**

Action Points

1. Make a list of the persons who had already achieved what you want.

2. Find ways to stay near with them. Join Club, attend talks, go to networking events, study groups etc.

3. Even if, you need to pay for, pay it anyhow. But it is the most powerful trick.

4. Stay away from people who are failures and also discourage others.

5. But pay anything to stay with them, who those have achieved something and also inspire others also to achieve.

Part-IV Become De-analyser

After explaining the importance of proximity to Sammy, we were returned directly to our office and I again started explaining to him another dark side of our psychology, which prevents us from taking actions. Some author, trainer called it as Paralysis of Analysis. I started with the following story.

Story of Tom and John

Tom and John are good friends. They were in same school, but Tom was very intelligent. He always stood first in the class. On the other hand, John was just an average guy. Mother of John always inspired him to study more and become like Tom. But John never obeyed his Mom.

Due to poor family conditions, John had to stop his study and started distributing newspapers to earn some money for his family, but friendship of those two never affected due to this ups and down.

After few years, Tom did his post-graduation from MBA institute, and joined his family business. At the same time John was planning to buy a car on loan to work as taxi man. Tom strongly recommended not to go for loan, but John continued with his decisions. After few years, John purchased another 2 cars and hired 2 driver to work for him. After few years, John managed to create successful travel company of the state and become billionaire. On the other hand, business of Tom was collapsing due to uncertain economic conditions.

I am not against getting good degree, but what went wrong with such intellectual guy, Tom.

Actually, most of the intellectual people make mainly 3 mistakes:

1. Analyse

2. Again analyse

3. And one last time – analyse

After analysing, they delay actions, and wait for the perfect time to come.

Now, understand the below chart, or thinking process of analyser which is in deep of his or her mind.

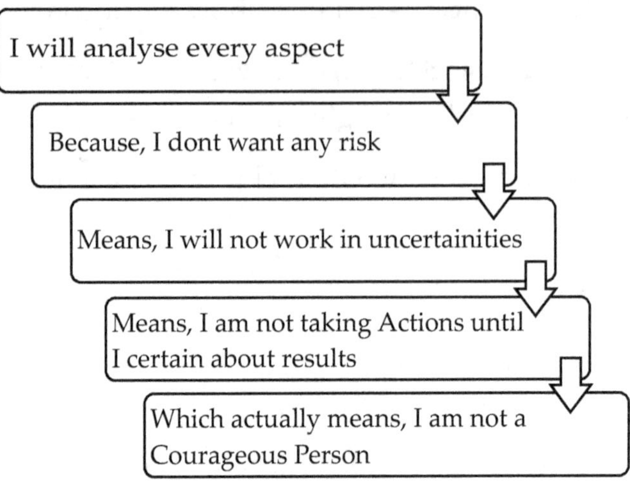

I am not against analysing. But, I am strongly against analysing which eventually results in inaction.

Actual thinking process should be like this

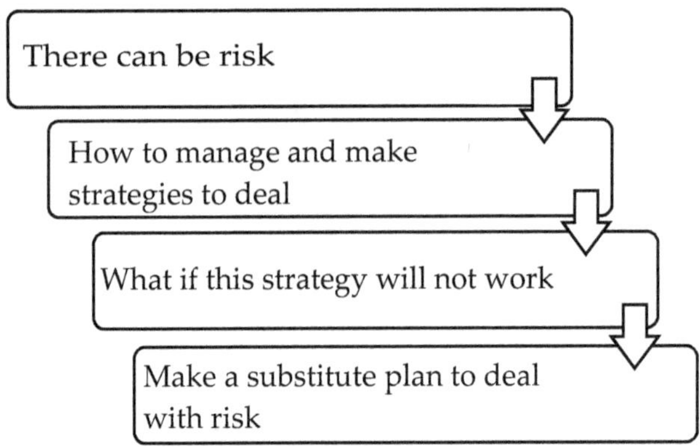

what I really want to suggest you through these diagrams is, use your intelligence to deal with adversities, not avoid them.

Remember,

> **"Actions can be planned, not perfection, but perfection always follow actions."**
>
> **–Harish Miglani**

The another reason of more analyses is that everyone wants perfection while planning.

If this holds true, you already loose the battle.

> **"If you look for perfection, you'll never be content."**
>
> **–Leo Tolstoy**

Action Points

If you apprehend any risks while analysing, please analyse to deal with the risks, because the road to success is always uncertain.

Part-V Fire Your Fears

On the 4th Tuesday, I asked Sammy to reach directly at my office. I started speaking to him…

After understanding the importance of beliefs, why (the reason), upgrading the proximity and becoming de-analyser, nothing can stop you from taking actions, but still, there may be situations where you tend to stop. The reason is that no one wants to change its comfort zone. The state of mind in which you used to remain from last several years sometimes can stop you from moving towards your goal.

Because there is still one enemy to be conquered. This enemy is none other than your own fears.

If you work on the four fundamentals explained in last 4 chapters of psychology, you will easily be able to beat that fear.

Fear is a negative emotion which generally leads to inaction.

However, if you won over disempowering beliefs and identified your TRUE WHY, you will definitely take actions, your TRUE WHY is the universal weapon to beat any negative emotions.

Let's understand it with example

Suppose you don't know how to swim and you are scared of swimming. Will you go inside the water? The answer will be NO in most of the cases. In another situation, your near and dear is fallen into the water. Now will you even think before jumping into the water. Because your TRUE WHY is very very large than your fears.

How Fears are developed?

1. It is the by product of disempowering beliefs.

    Suppose your parents forbids you not to take any food from strangers. That day onwards, every stranger will become suspect.

2. Personal experiences of negative happenings in the society.

For example, you know someone who started business and later on his business proved a failure, which resulted in huge losses. Later on, you may be in state of fear while starting business, because of this happening.

Some fears may be genuine and need to analyse and need to make strategies to deal with those unfavourable possibilities, but most of the fears are nothing more than just negative emotions.

I want to give an example here. Suppose a person is walking in the street and dog starts chasing him due to whatever reasons and ultimately attacks on that person. Now in future, this person will be scared of any dogs, although all dogs are not like that a particular dog.

> **"Fear defeats more people than any other one thing in the world."**
>
> **–Ralph Waldo Emerson**

> # Action Points
>
> ## HOW TO DEAL WITH FEARS?
>
> ### Step 1 : Identify
>
> - Identify all your fears related to a particular goal.
>
> - Write the possible worse impacts, if it is proved true.
>
> ### Step 2 : Relax and rationalise
>
> - Because fear is the anticipation of possible outcome, right now it is just an emotion. And to deal with any negative emotion, firstly take 5-10 deep breathes and relax, whenever it disturbs you.
>
> - Now research from the Google the possibility of worse outcome. For example, a person is scared of travelling in aircraft. Now what google says death rate due to aeroplane crashes is just 0.24 % per million flights based on the average of last 5 years.(source: google.com). On the other hand, everyday 1.25 million people die due to car accident in a year averaging around 3,000 per day worldwide, and car accident is the 9th leading cause of death (source google.com). It simply means, you are multiple times safe in the aircraft as compared to cars.
>
> ### Step 3: Expert Opinion
>
> After working on above 2 steps, if you really feel there is genuine fears, then take the help of experts. Suppose a person is ill, he should take the help of doctors to deal it,instead of taking stress, how I will survive?

7
CHAPTER

STEP-2 : THE MASSIVE ACTIONS

Part-I Set Your Goals

On 5th Tuesday Morning, I gave a blank sheet to Sammy, and asked him to fill it and write your goals.

And he wrote as-

A big house, a luxury car , bank balance and ………

I asked him,

It is very much possible, you will never achieve it.

He was surprised and asked Why?

I explained him that, many people confuse Wishes/ Dreams with Goals.

But my dear friend, there is a huge difference between Dreams and Goals.

Goals	Dreams/Wishes
These motivate you to work.	These doesn't motivate you to work
Actions can be taken on goals.	Actions can't be taken on Dreams/wishes.
There is certain deadline for Goals.	There is no such deadline for dreams/wishes

So NOW what you have to do is:

- Write your all Dreams

  Take time to write (few hours, 1 day or 2 days) Whatever dreams you have 100-200 or …. just write.

- Now take Your Every Dream and Write why for that Dream

  Why we have to find WHY, what is explained in the Chapter of Activating DMS.

- If you are not able to find WHY with any dream, then that means, that dream is not so important in your life. So, leave it for the time being, consider it afresh in future.

- CHOOSE that goal of yours which has a list of more reasons of Why and start working on that because this is most important for you.

- There are certain rules to set your goals:

    i.   It should be written

    ii. It should be certain

    iii. It should be fixed

    iv. It should have a certain deadline

    v.   Decide a list of tasks you have to perform for that.

    vi. Fix a certain time for analysing, whether you are approaching your goal or not.

Dream + Why = Goal

> **"A goal properly set is halfway reached."**
>
> **– Zig Ziglar**

How to Achieve

1. Goals Should have Deadline: Your goal should have a certain deadline. Eg. You want lose 10 kg, and you have planned to achieve in it within 3 months, so 3 months is the deadline here.

2. Goals should be Specific/Certain: Eg. In above example, if it's mentioned that you want to all lose 10 kg , then 10 kg is certain. Now if you want to lose

some weight, it is not specific/certain. And its chance of being completed on time also rises when it is specific.

3.   Goal should be Realistic: Eg. You want to lose your weight and you have planned to lose 10 Kg in a month. Although there is certainty as well as deadline, but is that goal realistic or Achievable?

Let brake it into small parts –i.e. 1Kg. in 3 days or 333gm in 1 day

Ask yourself: is that possible to lose approx. 330 gm everyday from 30 days?

Think with the same speed you will lose 30 Kgs. in 3 Months. Is this possible?

So, your goal should be realistic.

4.   **Sacrifice:** The main thing is that-

In order to get something, you have to give something.

You can't get anything free of Cost.

Suppose you want good health, then –

You have to give time to exercise

You have to sacrifice your taste

Suppose you want to get good marks, then-

You have to give time to study

So, for getting anything or to reach your Goal, write what you are going to sacrifice.

5. **Time Slot:** You have to remind yourself of your goals constantly.

    So, you have to read your goal sheet minimum 1 time every day, so as to make it stored in your subconscious mind.

    But, for this you have to allocate a dedicated time for this.

6. **List of Habits:** In order to achieve your goals, you have to develop certain new habits, i.e you have to come out of your comfort zone. You have to be comfortable in uncomfortable.

    E.g. You want to expand your business, but you hate travelling. Then you have to develop habit of travelling by loving it, enjoying it.

7. **List of Skills:** You also have to develop your skill set.

    E.g. You want to perform as singer in a singing concert, so you need to practice it. You should also have confidence to sing in crowd.

    Both things are required here:

    Practice + confidence.

    If you just practice it regularly at your home or somewhere else, then it doesn't work. You should have skill set to face audience.

E.g. You are a businessman, you want to make your company enter into 100cr club. Then, you are not only required to increase sales, but also you have to have skills to organise people of your company. You should have the skill of marketing, planning for your business and lots more.

8. **Make a List of Companions:** We have already mentioned in the Chapter of Proximity that you have to improve your proximity.

But the thing is that how to improve it?

You need to have proximity according to your goal, or those who have the same goal or who are on the path of that goal.

Make a list of these type of people, be in their company, or work with them.

For example, if you are in a Cement Industry and you want to increase your production or you want to scale up your business, then you should be in the proximity of manufacturers, may be of some other product, if you are not able to find cement manufacturer.

So, you have to think on the proximity of people you want to be.

> **"All who have accomplished great things have had a great aim, have fixed their gaze on a goal which was high, one which sometimes seemed impossible."**
>
> **—Orison Swett Marden**

9. **Possible Obstacles:** See, obstacles are bound to come. There is no one who is totally free from obstacles.

    So, make a list of possible obstacle which can arise.

    If you know in advance, which obstacles can come, then you can plan in advance, how to overcome it.

    What possible solutions are there.

    But, if you are not ready and if problem arises, then in that situation, you may not take the right decision.

10. **List of Beliefs Required to Achieve Goals:** For this, you have to believe that nothing is impossible.

    For e.g. If you want to lose weight, then you have to believe that losing weight is easy. But, if you think that once weight is gained can't be reduced, then in that case, you can't reduce it as you have a negative mindset in spite of a definite goal.

11. **List of Professionals/Experts you Need to Achieve your Goal:** In some goals, you may need the help of

professionals, because if your target is to reach the sales level of 1,000 crores for your business, you need a strong marketing expert.

So, you have to make a list of all the professionals you will need for achieving your goals.

Action Points

- Write your dreams first

- Plan to go out for 1 or 2 days

- Identify your why

- Make goals with the instructions given above

Part-II Break Your Goal into MAPs

The 5th Tuesday was going very long, and I allowed him to go to home around 6 p.m. but this time with homework. I gave a homework to him that you have to stay out of your current routine for the next 2 or 3 days, for setting up goals.

But Goal setting is of no use if it is not executed, so there was additional homework to break his goal into MAPs.

What is MAP?

MAP stands for Micro Action Points. There is a famous quote:

> **"Rome was not built in a day".**

This holds totally true, because whenever anything is achieved, it is not achieved due effort of 1 day or 2 days or 10 days.

The whole idea is that break your entire goal into micro goals, and then to achieve micro goals. You have to plan micro actions.

For example, suppose a person wants to write a book which is around 300 pages. He can plan in a way that I will write 1 page every day, or 2 pages every day. Basically, there is nothing to do with 1 page or 2 pages. It depends on what are the other priorities. Difference is that in later case, book will complete early as compared to former case.

> **"A goal without a plan is just a wish."**
>
> **–Antoine de Saint-Exupéry,**
> **writer and pioneering aviator**

One more thing that is going to happen is that suppose he chooses 1 page every day, the book is not going to take 300 days. It will take less than 300 days, but how?

I am telling you if writing 1 page everyday will become consistent, then internally such person will feel as achiever and this will create the positive reinforcement within his mind, which will in turn definitely go to increase the writing speed of that person.

On the other scenario, this person plans to write 50 pages every day, then there are more chances to get deviated from it. It is simply because writing 50 pages is not a micro action.

Our mind allows us to take micro actions easily, if it is a new thing. But it doesn't allow to take the new large actions.

What we have to do then?

We need to keep the directions right, because if the direction is right, we will definitely reach the goal.

Wait for Habits to Become

Another benefit of taking micro actions is that, it will become our habit soon. We will not use much will power to do it, then we can increase the activity.

Unless and until any activity becomes our habit, we have to use so much will power to accomplish it. But if it is a micro action, very less will power is going to be used.

Suppose a student wants to give any competition exam in the next 6 months. He wants to study his entire syllabus. Then he should start with 1 or 2 pages per day of every subject initially. When this will become habit, he can increase the coverage of syllabus slowly on the daily basis.

Another example of micro actions

Suppose a person wants to construct a building, then making a phone call to a contractor is a micro action, calling to architect is another micro action.

Action Points

1. Break your goal into micro actions first

2. Identify list of actions which you can take

3. Start taking those micro actions

    There will be certain things which you may not be able to do because of certain limitations. But, there will be many things which you will be able to do in spite of those limitations.

    For example, if a businessman wants to increase its revenue or sales, but he is not having the funds to spend on marketing, then he should go for networking and he can join networking events.

Part-III Find a Mentor

On 6th Tuesday, Sammy was very excited. He prepared his goal sheet. He also broke his goal into MAPs. He came up with the idea of creating online consultancy company that will give consultancy services to all MSME clients all over India, on matters related to GST.

Now, I was about to give a very important lesson to him, which is needed to understand for all people in the society.

When you prepare a goal sheet, it's ok. But, there may be some weaknesses in your action plans. So, who will review your action plans to achieve those goals?

At the stage of taking actions, before initiating any action, you need to take the help of a mentor to understand whether your action plan is right or wrong, or it needs some improvements.

Mentor is a person who is experienced to understand the action plan you created to achieve the goals you want. He knows what will work and what will not.

A mentor is a multi-dimensional person. He can evaluate your action plan from multiple angles, and he can also help to create one, if you are struggling to make this.

Almost everyone needs mentor. As you know, in ancient time also, when there were kings of the cities, they were also having gurus in the assembly hall of those kings, who used to give advice to those kings.

Who can be your mentor?

There are two types of mentor which will be very beneficial for you.

First ones are those who have achieved something in their life because they can guide you how to pursue goals, what strategies will make you succeed, etc. But, don't ignore the second ones, because they will be the trouble-shooter for you. They will guide you what is not going to work. They will always guide you how to avoid the wrong path. Yes, they are the ones who failed many times.

How to Chose Mentor

You review your goal sheet and go to part of goal sheet which tells you the list of skills and habits you need to learn.

> **"The best way a mentor can prepare another leader is to expose him or her to other great people."**
>
> **– John C. Maxwell**

For all those skills and habits you will need a mentor. It's not necessary for you to have paid mentors, you can find your mentors in your friend circle or even family also. Suppose you need to develop a habit to wake up early, you can take the help of a person usually wakes up in the early morning.

Likewise, if you need to improve your public speaking skills, you can take the help of the teachers, trainers in your circle.

If you don't get, find a role model according to the skill you need to develop. Let's again take the example of public speaking. You can go to youtube and watch videos of Ujjwal Patni, Tony Robbins, Robin Sharma, Sandeep Maheshwari, Jack Canfield and many more.

How to Select Paid Mentors?

Coaching by Coaches (one to many)	Coaches are those persons who shift or transform your mindset. They are the persons, who change the way you look at the situations around you. Role of Coaches is to bring the best out of you. This way is best for common problems.
Consulting by Consultants (one to one)	Consultants understand your problems on personal level and offer solutions to you, and work with you to deal with the problems you are facing.
Training by Trainers	Trainers train you for particular skill, like public speaking, sales trainer, digital marketing etc.

Nowadays, trainers and coaches synonym to each other. There are trainers who train you as well as change your mindset or transform the way you think.

Precautions

- One mentor at a time for one domain, because procedure of different mentors may be different, confusion always leads to inaction.

- Mentor will give you tips and tricks, but it is you, who actually have to implement, mentors can't work for you.

- Don't get emotional while taking advice. Take advice from those who are the experts in the topic on which you need advice. Don't take advice from family members or relatives who are not having the knowledge related to the topic.

Action Points

Find mentors according to the skills that you need to learn or the shift you really want in your mindsets. This entire chapter is full of solutions which can be very useful for you.

Part-IV Become Consistent

It was 7th Tuesday and this learning journey of 2 BIG STEPS was about to complete, and on that day Sammy was going to understand the most crucial aspect of 2 BIG STEPS.

After reaching, he told me how his life has started to turn now, and he was feeling very much confident. He started to take decisions, because he had identified his TRUE WHY.

> **"The best way a mentor can prepare another leader is to expose him or her to other great people."**
>
> **– Tony Robbins**

But, he was very much curious to know as to why today's learning is so important.

I started speaking…

There are so many good values. But, there is one father of all values that is consistency.

Suppose you made a goal sheet but you are not consistent on reading it.

You created MAPs, but you are not consistent on taking actions.

You learned the skills from mentor, but you are not consistent on practising it.

What will happen— every effort, every resource that you applied on goals will be wasted.

Your money invested will be wasted.

Your time spent on finding your why will be wasted.

Your time spent on preparing goal sheet will be wasted.

Sad, but true..

> **"Without consistency in actions, success is just a co-incidence".**
>
> **– Harish Miglani**

Yess, consistency is a seed and habits are the ultimate tree.

Now Listen Carefully

A person who is very fond of eating fried and oily food, will surely get health issues sooner or later. Even after knowing this fact it becomes very difficult for him to get rid of this habit.

But, if you become habitual to certain finest things, you can transform your life forever.

If you become consistent to exercise, your health will be awesome, even if you don't want.

If you become consistent to take Micro Action Points (MAPs), you will definitely reach your goal, even if you don't want.

Action Points

1. First, identify the habits you really want to develop

2. Then create MAPs for this habit

3. Remember, for developing the habit, you have to become consistent

4. Initially, you need to fix a very small slot to do it

5. For developing a habit, consistency of activity is the most important factor, not the quantum of activity

Part-V Gift of Obstacles

Transformation journey of 7 Weeks was about to end, and I asked Sammy, "This is my last warning to you, never think, if you follow all these steps, you will get momentum".

> **"It still holds true that man is most uniquely human when he turns obstacles into opportunities."**
>
> **– Eric Hoffer**

Obstacles are bound to come, doesn't matter who you are.

- Steve Jobs was once fired from his self-created company Apple.

- Mark Zuckerberg was once also rejected from WhatsApp.

- WhatsApp Co-founder Brian Acton was turned down for employment by both Twitter and Facebook in 2009.

But, I am not here just to preach you.

I am giving you the practical benefits of obstacles or problems.

Suppose you have planned to go out with family, and while sitting in the car, you got surprised when you saw the front tyre punctured. You started feeling apprehensive about the success of your planning.

Now, what is your state of mind in such situations, will tell whether you are a positive or negative person.

In the above case, think about one twist.

There was no puncture initially and you went out. After departing from your city, you observed that there is puncture. Then, what will you do?

Now tell

Which situation is better—first or second?

Remember

> **Some time, small obstacles are there to save you from big problems.**
>
> **– Harish Miglani**

Change the lens to see the problem not as problem, see it as an indicator. The problem is just indicating you that something went wrong. It gives you the caution signal and tells you that you have to be careful in the future. Simply put,

Something is not right, I have to take some actions.

A simple stomach ache may indicate that you have to be conscious while eating. If not, then some big problems can arise in future.

Do not see problem as problem. See problem as mentor. They are giving you feedback about the actions you are taking without any fee. They are guiding you about your plans.

Instead of avoiding a problem, always work on dealing with the problems because most money is made by those, who solve the problems of others.

Action Points

1. Write all the obstacles that may come.

2. Write what worse can happen with the obstacles

3. Rank the obstacles based on most worse as no. 1

4. Starting from rank 1, write at least 3 possible solutions/strategies to deal with them, when they arise.

5. Analyse the possible solutions and ready to take if required

At the end, I thank to all my readers for picking this book.

In the upcoming 2 chapters there are some free benefits for you.

QUICK NOTES TO READ DAILY

To get the free reminder tool, mail me @

2BIGSTEPSBYHM@GMAIL.COM

I will send you the crux of these entire 2 big steps journey in one sheet.

9
CHAPTER

UNLOCK THE OFFER

If you really want to make your journey easier, and want to connect with me one to one, them mail me your email id @

2BIGSTEPSBYHM@GMAIL.COM

I will send you PDF of MCQs, if you are able to answer it right, you will get free consultancy over the call.

www.ingramcontent.com/pod-product-compliance
Lightning Source LLC
LaVergne TN
LVHW041340200726

843509LV00009B/799